Birchington,
Now, Then and Gone Forever Volume II

A Birchington Roundabout publication

A catalogue record for this book is available from the British Library

ISBN 0-9553646-0-4

ISBN 978-0-9553646-0-0

Printed and bound in Great Britain by Hammond Press Ltd, 424 Margate Road, Ramsgate Kent

Contents

Introduction

Encouraged by the popularity of our first volume we have pleasure in taking you on another nostalgic pictorial journey through the village of Birchington, looking at the changes, both man-made and environmental, that have taken place over the last 120 years.

These pictures have been drawn from many sources including Birchington Roundabout readers who have generously donated their images for the enjoyment of others, and from the Birchington Heritage Trust which has over the years also acquired many pictures from local poeple. These donations are often accompanied by requests to make the pictures more available to village residents and the Birchington Roundabout is pleased to fulfil those wishes.

In volume II we show more of these changes, highlighting how many of our fields, ponds, cliffs and woods have truly gone forever. We also include some of the people who have lived in Birchington - the labourers, trades people, public servants, residents, visitors and the local people who have constructed and contributed to the environment we see around us today.

Proud generations have come and gone. People have married, had families and grown old, safe in the knowledge that Birchington was, and still is, a good place to live one's life as we benefit from the health giving sea air and nourishment from the fertile farm land. We hope this book will inform and entertain whilst giving a light-hearted glimpse of our wonderful heritage so easily taken for granted, much of which has now gone forever.

Stuart Horner
Birchington
September 2006

The overwhelming enjoyment of being beside the sea in Birchington can be seen on the faces of the Haig family and their friends in this unusually informal photograph from the 1890s: an early taste of the fun that would be had by thousands of visitors to the village's beaches over the decades to come.

In this picture of around 1900 The Square is shown in panoramic view. Whilst the Haigs giggled in their corsets down at Minnis Bay, rural matters continued at a leisurely pace at the heart of the village. All Saints' church and its landmark spire overlooks the daily labours and routines of village life.

Whilst a one horse powered wagon moves bales of hay under a warm sun, another one pauses outside the New Inn for a welcome drink (beer?) It would be nearly another decade before a drinking fountain is provided for the thirsty workers. Humanely, troughs were also to be provided for horses and dogs.

One of the earliest photos of Station Road, dated c1880, shows the ornate Dutch gables of Laburnum House. Built in about 1765 it was already over a 100 years old by the time this picture was taken. Opposite, a small row of trees shades another venerable property now long gone and featured on page 10.

126 years later and Laburnum House still stands proudly at the head of Station Road. Gone are the trees to the left of the building which presumably were Laburnum. Many trees grew along Station Road in the 19th Century - replanting in the 21st is returning the main shopping area to a more natural state.

Also taken in about 1880 this picture features another ancient building which was once a familiar site to villagers going about their daily lives in Station Road. Its small dormer windows and single storey suggest it might be considered as an early chalet bungalow, much loved in the village today.

By the turn of the century the house had been demolished, and it is recorded that this was much to some peoples' consternation. Half of the building we see today was used as the village Post Office. Behind this building was a small sorting office which is now the official office of the Birchington Parish Council.

In the early 1900s the horse was king, and rural Birchington was no exception. These faithful beasts were ploughing fields, pulling wagons and delivering the provisions to every corner of the community. Moving people between towns, to work or play, was also part of a horse's burden.

Some horses had to double up their duties. In 1900, our Fire Brigade was located behind Station Garage and these horses would not only be pulling day trippers and travellers' coaches but also the fire tenders. One speculates what would have happened if when pulling day trippers the horse got a whiff of smoke!

To keep the wheels and horses moving the village relied heavily on the blacksmith. Located opposite All Saints' church, Buddle's blacksmiths supplied this service for many years, starting in the 1890s. Mr Buddle is shown on the left. Mr Hinkley, in the centre, later took over the business.

Today the building can still be seen from the road, opposite All Saints' church, on the left hand side as you leave the village. Its location isn't by accicdent as the blacksmiths services were frequently required by the church. The main road location didn't do Mr Buddle's business any harm either.

This picture shows the Boxing Day hunt of 1909. Featuring in numerous photographs over the early part of the 20th Century, the popularity of the hunt confirmed Birchington's farming and rural connections. Some of the pictures were taken from first floor windows of the pubs which surround The Square.

This picture shows the Grant memorial drinking fountain being opened in June 1909. The fountain was a controversial matter at the outset. First suggested in 1900 to the Parish Council it was debated and delayed for nearly ten years. The Rev H A Serres conducted the service.

By the 1920s the motor bus was well established as a popular and safe mode of transport for visitors and workers alike. Motor buses became a common sight in The Square - which quickly became a terminus for the impressive vehicles as they rattled and lumbered towards the Thanet towns.

The bus driver in this picture has been persuaded to leave his open air cab to pose with some of his passengers before journeying on to Westgate, Garlinge and Margate. Note the manual horn to the side of his seat, no doubt little used in the light traffic of the day!

In about 1910 an elegant open top bus is seen leaving The Square heading towards Westgate and Margate, passing what would one day become the junction into Yew Tree Gardens. Luckily very little traffic, if any, is coming the other way as the bus moves sedately down the centre of the road!

Sixty years later an open top service was seen again but this time hugged the coast from Minnis Bay to Ramsgate Harbour. Generations of locals and visitors gained a birds' eye view of the coastline and sometimes a soaking! The service started in the summer of 1959 and continued for over 20 years.

The garage of Watson & Co at the junction of Canterbury Road and Park Lane opposite All Saints' Church, pictured in the 1920s. Established on the site for over 40 years, it started life behind an old cottage (shown on page 17) later gaining an access onto the Canterbury Road via the large gates shown.

Part of the boundary wall and railings still remain but little else to remind us of its long service to motor vehicles of the village. The site was redeveloped with private houses designed by John Brown Architect of Margate in the late 1970s. Happily the trees have survived into the 21st Century.

Watson & Co's yard, in the 1920s, situated on the corner of Park Lane. Happy workers pause from their labours repairing the growing number of motor vehicles which passed through the village every day. The trucks signage informs us that Watson & Co also delivered coal and coke nuts.

Watson & Co also repaired tractors and agricultural machinery for the local farmers. These fine examples were proudly parked and posed for this photograph in the 1920s. With no rubber tyres on the tractors, the journey back to the farm, probably Quex Farm, would have been across the fields.

Popular Minnis Bay in the 1950s, this photograph was probably taken from the roof terrace of the Minnis Café. The arched sign in the foreground advertises the cafe and the fine views it offered the day trippers, who were by now arriving in great numbers by car every summer to enjoy the sun, sea and sands of Birchington.

In the distance the Bay Hotel was still providing guests with a panoramic view of Minnis Bay into the early 1950s. While the day tripper continued to arrive by car in greater numbers the necessity for a parking attendant appeared to be vital to keep order, and judging by the neat row, with great success.

Having arrived at Minnis Bay in the 1920s visitors could pay to use a hut to change in, as this picture demonstrates. With the lack of railings and the huge drop to the sand, Health and Safety was obviously not an issue! Minnis Bay beach huts are now so popular that there is currently a seven year waiting list.

Eighty years later George Kup plays on the sand just below the promenade despite the inclement weather of a chilly May. George's mother took this picture which was judged as the winning entry in a Roundabout Competition. In the background we see that the promenade is now a safer place to stroll.

For hundreds of years people have enjoyed the sunsets at Minnis Bay, which have silhouetted the towers of Reculver. As this etching illustrates from 1800, the church and surrounding cliff have been greatly reduced by the elements over the centuries. The towers were preserved partly as landmarks for shipping.

The ancient stone towers are now a protected monument and form an historic backdrop to the horizon seen from Minnis Bay. Artifacts have been unearthed here including the grave of a Roman child. On dark stormy nights locals have reported the ghostly sound of a child crying. Probably just wind!

The Dip in the 1950s. In the far distance can be seen the reconstruction work of the promenade which was destroyed during the devastating storm surge of 1953. Also note the early location of the Minnis Bay sailing club which later moved nearer the Minnis Café.

Only a few extra houses change this view of Minnis Bay from the one in the 50s. Note the disappearance of the hedge running along the top of the bank, removed to save maintenance costs. The shelters remain stoically in position giving temporary relief from the easterly gales that often occur in June!

In 1897 a great storm wrecked the exhibition building in Minnis Bay. It was constructed in 1885, the brainchild of Arthur Rayden who chartered trains to bring people from London. He hoped they would purchase plots of land from him. It was soon rebuilt and used until 1905.

The green space adjoining the Dip has been a recreational area benefiting day trippers and residents alike for nearly a century. Recently a playground for young children has been created adding to the fun of this popular location close to the beach, but without the inconvenience of eating sandy sandwiches .

The Dip at the turn of the century looking like a sunken garden with its ornate steps and attractive hedges encouraging visitors to seek some shelter from the breezes on cooler days by the sea. In the bacground are the Victorian buildings known as the First Houses, which feature greatly in many photos of the time.

A plain grassed area now replaces the ornamental features of the Dip. The installation of goal posts now encourages more vigorous forms of relaxation. Riding one's bike at speed down the grassy banks is another popular pastime in the once genteel area of the Dip.

A view showing some of the earliest sea defences. Dating from around the early 1890s they proved little protection during the catastrophic storm of 1897. The picture seems to show the defences under construction but closer inspection suggests this was the finished article.

In 1919 the Swedish schooner The Valkyr ran aground off Minnis Bay. The cargo of sardines, salt fish and cork was soon liberated by locals as it spilled ashore in the heavy gales. The picture shows what's left of The Valkyr today. Inset shows the salvage workers completing the removal of the cargo.

The great storm of 1897 not only destroyed Mr Rayden's exhibition centre at the heart of Minnis Bay; it also tore away large sections of the coastal paths, walk ways and cliffs around the coastline. Here we see young children inspecting the space that was to become the boating pool, or the crabbing pool as we now call it.

In 2006 the coastal defences are more robust. The boating pool just seen on the left was constructed in the 1930s and is still intact today. Behind the row of beach huts were the distinctive alcoves built into the cliff in the 1890s, of which only one remains. These were constructed as recessed seating areas.

The soft chalk has eroded quickly in some areas leaving strange formations all along the coast. This aerial photo reveals the convoluted and curvaceous nature our cliffs once had. The cliffs often featured in photos and post cards with names such as *The Trouser Cliff, The Key Hole* and *King Canute*.

An aerial view reveals the Bay hotel in close up during the 1950s. Built in 1905 it provided quality accommodation overlooking Minnis Bay. In a basement to the right of the hotel was the popular Uncle Tom's Cabin bar. By the mid 1960s the hotel had gone and this prime site was developed to provide blocks of flats.

Ironically seaweed may have been partly responsible for the popularity of our beaches. In years gone by the access gaps were hand dug and enlarged by people keen to collect the seaweed for fertilizing the surrounding fields. The lime from the chalk cliffs was used in the building industry, the village once having two lime kilns.

These gaps became thoroughfares for everybody visiting the beach during the early part of the century and were gradually improved and made easier by constant use. Visitors wanting better beaches began to seek out easier access to other bays. Our obsession with the sea and sand had begun.

In this view the promenade was still on the drawing board, but when it arrived these natural curves gave way to a sharp concrete edge which was to stretch from Minnis Bay to Margate, with the exception of Epple Bay, by the end of the last century. This vital cliff protection has also become a popular cycle path.

Another view further along showing Cliff Road. A vast swathe of agricultural land reaches almost to the cliff tops held back only by the imperative of the motor car. During the 1960s these cabbage fields all but disappeared as Birchington's housing boom gained momentum.

The famous chalk stack, which came to be known as the Sentinel, in the 1930s possibly located near Grenham Bay. Two young lovelies cavort around the chalk edifice exemplifying the healthy feel that only Birchington's sun, sea and sand can give. Health and beauty were the watch words of the era.

In July 2006 the weather turned hot and our beaches took on a Mediterranean feel. Two local health fanatics eagerly volunteered to recreate the picture from the 1930s. Three quarters of a century later the cliffs may have changed beyond recognition - but youth is still energetic and eager to show off!

The bottom of Beresford Gap in 1900. Raised beach huts line the slip way giving bathers a drier and more grandiose vantage point to contemplate another swim. The huts appear to be of timber construction which was a departure from the earlier canvas models.

Possibly one of the last pictures of The Beresford Hotel. Taken in the 60s it shows the completed concrete apron now obliterating the sandy beach that had been enjoyed by many in the past. The hotel burned down in 1968 during demolition. The site was eventually developed as a small estate of Georgian style houses.

During the First World War the Beresford Hotel was utilised as a hospital. This picture taken in 1917 shows wounded men tended by serene nurses, enjoying the pleasant shade from the pine trees on the cliff top lawns; a far cry from the horrors of France and trench life. Inset taken at Christmas 1917.

This sombre photograph shows some of the staff who were caring for the wounded at the Beresford Hotel in 1917. Other large properties took in wounded soldiers during the First World War including The Thicket in Cross Road, St Mary's in Beach Avenue as well as Quex House.

Pupils of The Bay College in the Minnis Bay area c1900 pose in their smart straw boaters. The school educated a wide age range of boys, although one chap (back row far right) seems to be heading into middle age! His now bankrupt parents no doubt cursed the day they suggested his education by the seaside!

This photo from c1920 shows a visiting clergyman and his wife bringing the church choir to the seaside. Note the odd range of dress, from winter coats, baggy swimwear, jumpers; and is the vicar still wearing his tight rubber swimming cap?

Empire Day celebrations in 1927. Local school children dress up in costumes from around the Empire and through the ages. Careful study of the background shows they are seated in one of the display rooms at Quex House museum, in front of one of the famous dioramas of African wildlife.

The Birchington Guild of Players pantomime of 1954. This production was presented from the old Church House situated on the corner of Kent Gardens and the Canterbury Road. The name of the panto is open to speculation as the record for that year has been lost. "Look behind you!" I hear you cry.

In the 1950s local man Peter Dadds was proud to be part of the Kent constabulary. Fifty years ago the uniforms appear basic and somewhat flimsy and the only real protective equipment on show is a trusty whistle on a chain. Incredible to think that law and order could be maintained with a wind instrument and healthy respect.

During the winter of 1959 The Square was covered in deep snow. A police officer keeps a watchful eye on pedestrians and traffic as they pass through the village. The distinctive police box on the right of the picture stands out as a reassuring statement of authority at the heart of the village.

The Birchington Silver Band has been a part of village life for over 70 years, emerging in the 1930s. This photograph could be older, thought to show some of the first musicians who got together to play for the village at celebrations and public events at the turn of the century. Moustaches were mandatory!

By 1935 Margate Borough had gobbled up the village of Birchington into its corporation. Pictured above is what would now be called a PR exercise by the portly Mayor and Mayoress of Margate. They are reluctant participants in our "Beating the Bounds" celebrations. A comical caption would be too easy!

In 1905 Major and Mrs Powell Cotton married in Nairobi and upon their return to the village in 1907 (a working honeymoon) they were welcomed at the railway station. Joyously they were pulled by their employees and local residents triumphantly along Station Road for all to cheer and congratulate.

Upon their return the happy couple celebrated with the village and enjoyed a huge party in the grounds of their home. " Welcome Home - Long Life and Happiness" was emblazoned across the front of Quex House and everybody had the opportunity to dress in their best clothes and mingle with the toffs.

Sheep dipping on the Quex Farm Estate in 1913. With the First World War on the horizon rural life around Birchington continues as yet unaffected by world events. Within 18 months Quex House would be opened as a hospital for wounded and invalid soldiers from France with Mrs Powell Cotton as Commandant.

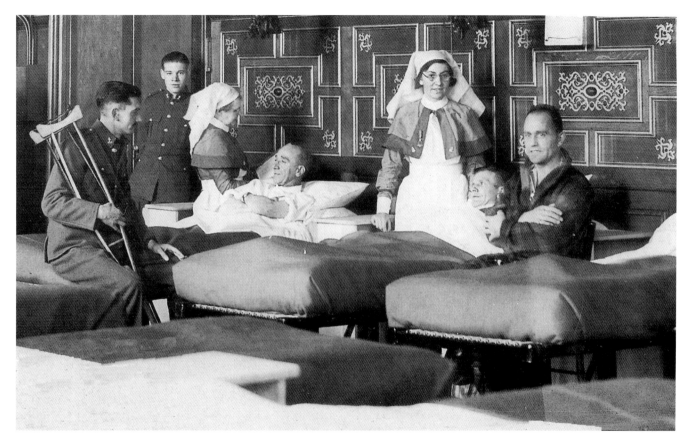

In 1917 patients and staff are shown in one of the rooms that had been converted into rather luxurious wards at Quex House. Armaments surrounded the injured, one being *Napoleon's Cannon*, captured by the French in Egypt in 1797. Located in the hall, it is thought that Napoleon used it as a signal gun.

Park Lane School Birchington in the 1920s. The children sit as still as they can with pencils poised, but the slow shutter of the camera struggles to freeze some of the fidgeting boys in time. The painted brick walls suggest a prison-like environment, which these country boys surely agreed with in the summer.

In 1931 the desks haven't changed and the faces still look solemn, but less fidgeting is evident as order is being maintained by the Head Master Mr Charles Laming (Laming Road was named after him). Perhaps his presence ensured that the apostrophe was placed in the correct location on the chalk board?

Better light was to be had in the playground, the pupils probably glad to escape the classroom for a while, so in 1935 the boys at Park Lane School line up in a football team style arrangement. Folded arms and determined faces suggest a pride in their school, which was by now over 80 years old.

Signs of a less formal style of schooling were emerging at Park Lane during 1953 as this picture may suggest. The little ones are re-enacting the nursery rhyme Humpty Dumpty; Humpty has yet to experience his great fall, so the King's men wait patiently in their blazers, sandals and paper caps for the inevitable plunge.

The Park Lane School photo of 1955 and at last smiling is on the curriculum, many of the children making full use of this new found skill. The school was by now nearly 110 years old. Generations of children had passed through its Victorian doors and endured the draughty winters and stifling summers - to good effect.

The somewhat distracted Birchington Brownies and leaders, Esther Eastland and Doris Wilkes, of 1956 celebrating with their May Queen. Dancing around the Mapole was a regular event for the Brownies until the late 1970s and many residents of the village still remember these celebrations with fondness.

1910 and 'the school run' had a different meaning for children of this era; many would have run down this road at the end of a school day. In this picture motor cars do not yet pose a threat to our children through speeding or fumes, although it appears that a little horse pollution had to be tolerated!

One side of Park Lane hasn't changed much in the last 96 years., but now extensive public housing dominates the right hand side of the lane. Built in the 1950s the estate linked Park Lane with Park Road via Linington Road. The location gave children good access to the school, shops and recreation ground.

1933 and a "look-alikey" scoops first prize in Birchington's second ever carnival. Possibly category: *best comical ladies' costume*? In the year Amy Johnson crossed the Atlantic from Pendine Sands in South Wales to the United States, the judges would have been stunned by the resemblance to the real aviator!

By 1934 the carnival tradition had taken root in the village. Although only two previous parades had taken place, people were entering into the spirit of this popular annual summer event with gusto. This picture shows a bewildering mix of costumes and you may find it difficult to spot the invisible man.

During the early years of WW II The Vicar, Rev Maurice Granville Sharp, formed a small school in the old Church House for the children who were not evacuated. Records show he was ably assisted in this venture by Miss Le May, Miss Phillips, Mrs Beadle and many others including the Rev Mr Reeves.

In 1969, we find Church House is again home to a school, called St Gabriel's, under the kindly steward-
ship of Miss Panter. Sadly the infant school was soon to close due to the building's redevelopment. The
boy in front, holding his friend's hand, grew up to become a Chairman of the Parish Council!

This photograph shows the view many people would have had as they approached Birchington from the Canterbury direction in the 1890s. The slopes each side of the village pond were there to make it easier for animals to have a drink or cool off. The pond was partly owned by Court Mount Farm.

By 1910 the pond had been tamed with safer iron railings. During the cold winters of this period the pond froze regularly, partly due to its shallow depth. The pond would survive for only another 23 years before it was finally filled and disappeared under concrete when the Canterbury Road was widened in c1933.

In the 1920s Birchington business woman, Mrs Hudson, had two shops built as an investment on the Canterbury Road opposite the pond. Due to financial constraints the properties were constructed without upper floors. Later as her businesses became established and successful her empire enlarged and so did her shops.

75 years later Mrs Hudson's shops still stand proudly on the Canterbury Road. With their distinctive rolled wrought iron canopies and ornate pillars they are a fine testament to a woman who succeeded in a man's world with entrepreneurial skills ahead of her time. Inset: Mrs Hudson in later life.

The picture for this post card was taken in the early 1930s showing the newly planted trees and grass verge indicating the recent burial of the village pond. A motor car is quickly on the scene of the crime, as a picture of the new road is taken for the record. Even more poignant is the post mark on the card - 2nd September 1939.

In 2006 driving or just crossing the Canterbury Road is not for the faint hearted. Lorries thunder along oblivious to the sedate heritage buried beneath their wheels; whilst contributing to the high levels of pollution in The Square. A permanent pollution monitor will be installed in the village in late 2006.

No 37 Canterbury Road in the 1950s - W J Powell's general store; handy for provisions for anyone living on this side of the village. The side of the house is painted ready for an advert - as yet unwritten. The signs which are visible refer to Brook Bond Tea and Player's cigarettes - a staple diet at the time!

The house is still standing today with its blank advertising space still waiting for a snappy slogan. The property is now fully residential with the shop windows and side door removed; although a faint outline can still be seen on the side wall, little is left to remind us of the thriving general store which traded for so many years.

Crescent Road at the turn of the century. This gently curving road links two of the oldest thoroughfares in Birchington - Station Road and Albion Road, both featuring on a map of 1688. The delightful lamp post has sadly long gone. The wagon to the left is on a delivery while a horse and trap await a passenger.

Counting the nine first floor windows of these crescent houses confirms they haven't changed hugely over the last 100 years, although the German air force did attempt some structural alterations to the properties during WWII when a Messerschmitt 109 crash landed in the back garden of a house close by.

At a cost of £28,000 Birchington got a new library in 1967. The first public library in Birchington was opened in 1936. It was situated in Station Road next to our popular Indian takeaway *Tandoori Nite*, in a similar large semi-detached house. To save public money it doubled up as the local rates office.

In 2006 the library was extensively refurbished. New fixtures, fittings, seating and shelving have been installed. Internet linked computers, DVD rentals and coffee machines give the library a 21st Century feel. Long serving librarian Heather Letley supplies a young book worm with more food for the holidays!

A post card of Minnis Road showing the Roman Catholic Presbytery during the First World War. During that war, it was used to house soldiers, one of whom wrote on the back of the card "it's a rotten place - all broke". The picture also shows the two malt houses that stood at the rear of the site until the 1950s.

During WWII the church forged friendships with the US Airmen at RAF Manston. These friendships bore fruit when the temporary wagon shed purchased in 1908, began to fall apart in 1959. The American servicemen helped to rebuild the old church, transforming it into the lovely Italianate building we see today.

Gordon Square in 1914, located at the eastern end of Kent Gardens. Recorded on maps of 1886 the square of 20 *two up two down* cottages was named after Gordon of Khartoum. During WW II lucky number seven had its cellar converted into a steel reinforced air raid shelter; possibly shared by others in the square.

Only recently there have been changes to Gordon Square, some of the cottages had their views obscured by the the new Medical Centre. Also, several new houses have been added to the the end of one row changing its symmetrical neatness for ever. This view was taken from the Medical Centre car park.

Some houses in Cross Road enjoyed a fine sea view in the early years of the road's development. Careful inspection reveals that parking was not a problem in Cross Road during the 1920s as one simply used the car park (cliffs) opposite. To describe the road as *unmade* would be a compliment to this dirt track!

Cross Road today and all the weeds, bumps and hollows have given way to flat bitumen *Blacktop*. Parking isn't as easy as it was in the 1920s but not as difficult as it is in some parts of the village. The gaps between all the properties have now been filled in, giving very little chance of any sea views.

Epple Road looking towards the railway bridge in about 1930. The hand made rustic fence encloses the gardens which were later to be sold off to provide building plots and a wider road. Inset picture suggests the Victorian post box has been moved further along into Alpha Road since this picture was taken.

Flint Terrace on the left of this picture has been a silent witness to decades of passing trains and pedestrians. Built in 1848 the builders could never have imagined in their wildest dreams that one day each would have a satellite dish attached to the wall receiving pictures from around the world.

Pictured in 1910, the box section Railway Bridge spanning Epple Road has stood the test of time and still takes the strain of the train many times a day. It has out lived the steam train by 40 years; the first ones arrived in 1863 and the last passed over it in 1962 shortly after electrification of the line in 1959.

Today the smart iron railings have vanished, possibly to help the efforts of WWII. The property on the right hand side replaced a Victorian cottage in 2005. During the 1960s the owner of this cottage kept budgerigars in an aviary adjoining the property giving the general area an exotic ambience.

Pictured in the 1920s is the somewhat austere, brick built property which once housed the lifeboat for the Coast Guard Station which was based at Epple Bay. Built in the late 1800s its unusual wedge shaped window on the sea facing side allowed the coast guard to keep watch in two directions.

Today we see that the Coast Guards Master's House to the left is still intact, but the boat house has gone. In 1987 an uproar was caused in the village when the boat house was earmarked for redevelopment. Despite many protests it was eventually sold and demolished ending over 100 years of history.

The brick fields of Epple Bay c1910. For such a small area Epple has seen more than its fair share of change over the years. Whilst in the ownership of the Powell Cotton Estate the area was stripped of its top soil which was formed into bricks, sun dried in situ and had 'PC' stamped on each - for Powell Cotton.

Epple Bay early 1900s showing the landmark retaining wall (surely constructed of PC bricks) probably needed to improve stability after the removal of so much top soil. The Coast Guard Cottages and boat house can be seen to the right. Obviously a popular location for the annual Punch and Judy convention!

Viewed today in panoramic aspect it's easier to see where all the soil for the bricks came from. *Epple Bay Avenue* and *Ocean Close* (with its excellent view of the Thames Estuary!) now sit in the shallow dip of the 'worked out' brick fields at Epple Bay, but sadly not one property is constructed with Powell Cotton bricks.

The fortress-like retaining wall eventually gives way to the narrowest and most imposing slipway to our beaches. Maps of the 1880s show another cutting through the cliffs to the right but this was filled in. Early maps also show a chalk stack at the centre of the bay which was dynamited to make way for the promenade.

Queen Bertha School in the 1920s. Birchington's scholastic endeavours and enviable location produced many private educational establishments. In 1929 Miss C M Hunt and Miss E Randall-Harris began a successful school for 'genteel young ladies' who wore distinctive gold and scarlet uniforms.

The school was sold and demolished in 1959 and the site developed. Backing on to the golf course the bungalows run along between the railway line and the Canterbury Road. Confusingly some have Westgate telephone numbers but Queen Bertha is definitely a Birchington monarch with an educational bloodline!

From the Canterbury Road facing East is this rear view of the cottages of St James' Terrace in the 1950s. The large Victorian building was a well known landmark visible from land and sea for many years, yet another substantial property demolished and replaced with a block of flats.

The neat cul-de-sac of Tudor Close now sits where the 'For Sale' sign stood. Access on to the Canterbury Road can be difficult, and modern traffic conditions would probably not allow such development to gain planning permission today. The chimneys of the cottages in St James' Terrace are still just visible.

Looking back towards the village in the 1950s reveals the way nature was once tolerated right up to the road's edge. The advertisement for Dreamland appears to occupy virtually the entire wall of the end cottage of York Terrace possibly giving the owner a small income?

With nature now retained behind garden walls and curbstones the Canterbury Road sweeps into the village. On the right the gable end of York Terrace can just be seen now without its huge Dreamland advertisement, removed long ago as its view was obscured by the new bungalows.

East End Farm at the top of Epple Bay Road in the 1920s. The property was run as a dog kennels for many years up to the 1960s. The distinctive and hard-wearing railings feature in many photographs spanning nearly 80 years. The entrance to Birchington Hall can just be seen in the distance to the left.

The farm house was demolished and the road widened in the 1950s, leaving little evidence of the once leafy junction down to Epple Bay. The land to the right hand side was built upon in the 1990s and once again motor cars and buses have gained the lion's share of the road, with small pavements to each side.

Approaching The Square on the right hand side is Yew Tree Gardens. Pictured is Yew Tree House demolished in the early 1960s to make way for new homes. Birchington had a large number of modest detached houses with over-generous gardens and many eventually supplied building land in the late 20th Century.

Yew Tree Gardens today shows a good example of the more efficient use of land, providing much needed homes for a growing population; a routine that was to be repeated around the village many times. Another example is seen at nearby Birchington Hall where Birch Hill Park estate now stands.

Birchington Hall in 1900, probably built in the late 1700s although a large house is shown on this site on very early maps. In the 1870s the house was occupied by Thomas Gray and his wife who were great benefactors to the village giving generously to the church and local community all their lives.

The property was sold at public auction in 1917 and purchased by the Baptist Church to become known as 'Spurgeon's Homes for Children'. When the site was again redeveloped to become the Birch Hill Park estate in the 1980s, the builders discovered two deep wells which dated from the 1700s.

This aerial view of Spurgeon's explains some of the changes which affected the site during its transition to a residential estate. The bottom right hand corner shows Park Road. Some of the main blocks were converted to flats and the houses to the top right of the picture remain today forming part of Brandon Way.

The chapel stood right at the back of the site to one side, but despite its tucked away location it played a central role for the children and staff of the home. The inset picture shows the attractive polished wood floors, plain seating arrangements and its overall uncluttered design.

To the left of the Methodist Church in The Square in 1896 Mr J Brooks, wife and son stand proudly outside their shop, apparently joined by a couple of jolly customers, whilst others peep out from inside. A wonderful snapshot of times past, showing that tastes in sweets and chocolate haven't changed much in over 100 years.

Sadly nothing remains to link today with the past except for the building itself rendered and painted many years ago to hide the alterations from shop to house. The large opening at the front, now bricked up, leaves no mark, no longer advertising the fancy tobacco or delicious Fry's chocolate!

The Methodist Church today. Built in 1830 it houses one of only three public clocks in the village, thought to be originally from the old Margate Pier and installed at the time of construction. The other two public clocks are on All Saints' Church and Quex Park stable block.

A close-up of the mechanism reveals the robust, almost agricultural, construction. The clock has not worked continuously over the years but in 1902 it was set working to commemorate the coronation of Edward VII. In 1976 Royal Marines scaled the tower to repair the hands and mechanism. The clock is now electrically driven.

From the Methodist Church tower, in 2006, wide views of the centre of the village can be gained. This aspect is looking west towards Park Lane and shows the neat rows of public housing. The first Council houses arrived in Birchington in 1927 along the Canterbury Road. Many are now privately owned.

Looking towards St Nicholas at Wade in 2006. In the foreground to the right is the roof of Grove House and the garden where Knotts Coach Works once stood (see page 132). All Saints' Church, which has the only wood shingled spire in Thanet, stands proudly overlooking The Square as it has done since the 13th Century.

This picture taken in the 1920/30s differs little from today from the point of view of buildings, with the exception of chimney stacks that have been removed and small extensions added. The lack of motor cars and buses gives a clue to the date; although the picture may have been taken on a Sunday.

In 2006 we see that The Powell Arms has been rendered and painted and Lloyds TSB Bank has possibly been re-roofed, after its 100 years of weathering. Interesting to note that the owner of the house in the foreground has finally managed to shut the window!

Panoramic view across Yew Tree Gardens, in 2006, showing the parade of shops built in the 1950s, and the car park of the Smugglers' Restaurant which, until 1930, was a private house called Evergreen, belonging to the Neame family. There is no evidence of smuggling activities here, but who knows?

These panoramic pictures were taken from the Methodist church tower which rises up above the chapel to be one of the highest view points around the village. The present chapel was opened on Thursday September 16th, 1830 and is now a Grade II Listed Building. Methodism in Birchington dates without interruption back to 1778.

On the right of this picture is Knott's Coach works in the 1880s, located for many years behind Grove House, shown on the left. The Knott family also ran a coach building business located in The Square, which later became the site of Jenner's garage.

In 2006 Grove House's distinctive 17th Century Dutch gable has survived into the 21st Century. The iron wall ties formed with the initials I M have fulfilled their function well - holding the cottage together for over 300 years. The building on the right was once a forge, possibly where the cart wheels were rimmed.

This excellent picture of the International Stores in The Square from the 1920s clearly demonstrates the company policy on smartness and cleanliness. The regimented window displays are echoed by the staff as they pose proudly outside their shop below the advertisements for margarine and exotic teas.

The International Store was eventually rebuilt and latterly Brills D.I.Y centre arrived in the village during the 1970s. The neat window displays showing tins of prime meats and bags of flour so proudly displayed in the windows of The International Stores have been replaced with tins of primer and bags of filler!

Next door but one, pictured here in the mid 1960s, was the Coffee Lounge. Owned for many years by Mr and Mrs William White (inset) known to regular customers as Bill and Jessie. Their ownership coincided with the Mods and Rockers era who parked their machines opposite and drank endless cups of delicious frothy coffee.

Thirty years later and the Coffee Lounge is now called the *Village Square Caf-a* but still provides welcome snacks and hot beverages. The 'cafe culture' has changed over the years; the 1960s customer enjoyed the facilities until 11pm but now the pubs fulfil this late service and provide endless pints of frothy beer!

Located prominently on the corner of Station Road and Albion Road, appropriately named George Gardener advertises his seeds, corn and flour. Built in the 1930s its ornate facia, Tuscan style columns and pedestals, lend it a classical air of quality unusual for a village greengrocers.

Today the building is used as one of the many estate agents in the village, but still stands out against the ordinary brick-faced properties around it. Its ornate fascia and distinctive shape forms a prestigious entrance to the beginning of Albion Road which started life as a humble footpath in the 17th Century.

Heading down Station Road we would have found the Bijou Fish Saloon, home to one of Birchington's many industrious business people of the last century. Mr Castle had numerous businesses including the donkey rides on the sands at Minnis Bay. Inset is his daughter, Edna, 'parking' one of his assets at the rear!
.

A man of many talents and costumes, Mr Castle was for many years also a chimney sweep, who would often attend weddings to administer good luck, and a children's entertainer dressed as a clown. He could often be seen shrimping locally, and to top it all, was a talented accordion player in his spare time!

The Wayside Café c1925, a well known focal point of Station Road. Its bungalow design would have made it stand out, set as it was amongst the tall Victorian houses. For many years painted wooden parrots welcomed the customers, many people today can still recall the brightly coloured birds.

In 2006 to the right and left of the picture we see ghosts of the past. A part of the roof of the Wayside cake shop remains intact after nearly 80 years, a testament to good building practice, and the Harbour Bakery still shades its window displays. A machine for parking tickets replaces the advertising A-board.

This detailed snapshot of Albert Golder's shop during the early 1900s shows us a catalogue of the tools available at the time to village gardeners and handymen. The racks of British-made spades, shears and hoes, watering cans and buckets, have now surely rusted away, having kept local gardens neat for 80 years.

61 Station Road today. With the domination of the DIY super stores, sadly very few independent iron-mongers still exist, and in those stores very few British-made tools can be purchased. Maybe the off-licence can offer some solace. Should we raise a glass to salute the passing of the Ironmonger for ever?

This picture of Chad Taxis in the 1940s, sandwiched tightly between the Wayside Café and Simmonds Builders, gives us a glimpse of everyday life in Station Road during the transitional period when push bikes, hand carts and the latest smart motor cars existed happily alongside each other in Birchington.

Eighty years later and part of the roof of the Wayside cake shop still looks attractive in the 21st Century, a rare survivor, all else having been replaced by plain modern buildings. Bereft of charm or character, these commercial ventures first brought Woolworths to the village and later the Co-op store we see today.

"S. G. Court Dispensing Chemist" says the distinctive sign above the door of 69 Station Road. Pictured in the 1920s, Courts has been a welcome sight for villagers for decades, supplying generations of ailing residents with its coloured bottles of ointments, lotions, potions, peptics, laxatives and antiseptics!

In 2006 the building is very different, with its generous double frontage. Today the shop has roller shutters to protect these windows every night, a far cry from the more law abiding times when few would think of raiding a village chemist, only those desperate for out of hours Brylcream or Sanatogen!

Station Road looking towards Dog Acre in the 1930s. On the right the trees denote the entrance to Woodford House School, which existed for nearly 70 years. The founder, Mr H A Erlebach, tragically lost three sons in World War I and donated the recreation ground in Park Road to the village in their memory.

In 2006 the shops look similar at first glance. The much maligned white van has now replaced the open flat bed truck, but in their time both have fulfilled the same needs of shops and traders, supplying goods to Station Road, one of the best village shopping facilities in Thanet.

Pictured in the 1930s are two of the large Victorian semi-detached properties of which there were six pairs originally. This side of Station Road was predominantly residential until the 50s and 60s. Pressure for more shops led to the eventual demolishing of four of the pairs for the valuable sites to be redeveloped.

In 2001 Station Road underwent a partial refurbishment with new paving, street lights, cycle racks and the planting of young Birch trees, echoing Station Road's residential beginnings. The trees were unwittingly planted close to where the trees once grew in front gardens of the large Victorian houses.

The long and varied history of this building in Station Approach, which started life in the 1880s as the cycle works, is nicely illustrated by this picture from the 1930s. E T Fasham Ltd provided general provisions including the ubiquitous Bovril, with tea rooms above and an estate agent trading alongside.

In the 70s Bob Hales' second hand furniture shop flourished; then John Mann, editor of *The Birchington Post*, opened a stationers. Within the last 10 years the premises has housed Birchington Fabrics, the Mobility Centre and currently, after extensive refurbishments, the wine bar has taken up residence.

In the 1880s the *Bridge Houses* were constructed in fine Victorian style close to the railway station and shops. Occupants were able to benefit from 'a convenient location, close to all amenities and facilities' as a contemporary advertising pamphlet enthuses.

Today some of the houses have actually become amenities themselves having been converted to shops over the years. The attractive false balconies and front gardens are now banished forever. A young lady cyclist passes close by where it is reputed ladies' cycles were invented by George Cousins over 100 years ago (page 152).

Crossing the bridge over the railway line into Lyell Road during the 1920s we see a rare winter aspect of the renowned Bungalow Hotel, possibly not fully booked at this time of year! Behind the Hotel is the roof line of Grenham House School emphasising the Hotel's unique single storey construction.

Taken in 2005 this contemporary winter view shows how a similar light snow fall has been affected differently by the motor car in comparison to the hooves and footprints of an earlier era. Bierce Court replaced the unique 106 year old Bungalow Hotel in 1986.

This picture from the 1920s of the roundabout at the top of Beach Avenue demonstrates how even the mundane can be made delightful, with its attractive white painted railings, neat flower bed and ornate gas lamp. The first gas lamps were installed in the village in 1876 at a cost of about £3 each.

Ironically in 2006 when traffic levels have reached saturation point, we find the roundabout almost indistinguishable from the road surface, four plastic bollards stand guard around the lanky street light and the unambiguous sign from the 1920s has been replaced by confusing symbols.

An unusual rear view of St Mary's Convalescent Home taken from Rossetti Road during the 1920s. The Chapel is in the foreground, with its sparse interior shown in the inset photograph. Two sensible perambulators sit forlornly outside in the fresh air; no doubt a popular healthy option for babies at the time.

St Mary's Convalescent Home in August 2006, from Rossetti Road showing the early stages of demolition. The building had remained empty and derelict for nearly two years before these works commenced. Another sad end to a long history of caring. To be replaced by yet another block of flats.

A testament to the health giving properties of Birchington - Miss Vida Bates in 2006, aged 96, has lived in the village for over 50 years. Inset picture of Vida aged 2. She has been involved with many aspects of village life including The Birchington Guild of Players from 1954, The Birchington Historical Society and is a "Friend of Quex". A much respected person who is well known for her indomitable spirit and determination, she is an inspiration to many half her age. When asked if she would partake in this book she warned us that it must not interfere with her keep fit class!

Parish and Heritage Trust archivist Miss Jennie Burgess stands beside one of the displays in the Birchington Heritage Museum. Jennie took on the job of Parish Archivist in 1985 and soon discovered there was a village as well as a church history in the archives. Now the sharing of this history with the community is one of her many passions. Under the guidance of Derek Raven the Heritage Trust was formed in 2002, and to this focal point came more history of the village, offered by local people in the form of memories, stories and photographs. Birchington's past is in safe hands and surely future generations will look back and see that less of our history has gone for ever.

Photographic credits and bibliography

The author is indebted to the following for the use of their photographs in the production of this book:

The Birchington Heritage Trust
Mr Mark Goddard
Many Birchington Roundabout readers and local residents.
All other photographs are from the Birchington Roundabout's collection.

The author is also indebted to Parish Archivist Miss Jennie Burgess whose wide knowledge of "all things Birchington" has been invaluable and without whose patience and enthusiasm this book would have been much the poorer.

Bibliography:
The Ville of Birchington by Alfred T Walker published 1981
Kelly's Directories 1883-4, 1934, 1938 and 1951

All reasonable steps have been taken to ensure the correct people are credited for the use of their photographs but any issues arising can be addressed to the author at 25 Alpha Road, Birchington, Kent CT7 9EG who will be happy to make corrections for any future editions.